D0578781

ENERGY
Revolution

Hydrogen
Running on Water

Niki Walker

Crabtree Publishing Company
www.crabtreebooks.com

Crabtree Publishing Company

www.crabtreebooks.com

Coordinating editor: Ellen Rodger

Series editor: Carrie Gleason

Project editor: L. Michelle Nielsen

Editors: Rachel Eagen, Adrianna Morganelli

Production coordinator: Rosie Gowsell

Production assistant: Samara Parent

Art director: Rob MacGregor

Photo research: Allison Napier

Consultant: Canadian Hydrogen Association; John Tak, President and CEO, Hydrogen & Fuel Cells Canada

Photographs: Ulana Switucha/Alamy: p. 27 (bottom); Photofusion Picture Library/Alamy: p. 21 (top right); AP/Wide World Photo: p. 17 (bottom), p. 18 (top), p. 19 (top); Dane Andrew/ZUMA/Corbis: cover; Fabrizio Bensch/Reuters/Corbis: p. 31 (bottom); Bettmann/Corbis: p. 23; Corbis: p. 3 (bottom left); Hulton-Deutsch Collection/Corbis: p. 24; Issei Kato/Reuters/Corbis: p. 5 (bottom right); Morteza Nikoubazl/Reuters/Corbis: p. 6; Bob Sacha/Corbis: p. 11 (top); Joe Skipper/Reuters/Corbis: p. 15 (top right); Ted Soqui/Corbis: p. 20 (bottom); Paul A. Souders/Corbis: p. 4; George Steinmetz/Corbis: p. 7 (bottom); CP/Abaca Press/Olivier Douliery: p. 13 (top); CP/Rex Features: p. 21 (middle); DOE/NREL-Jack Dempsey: p. 12 (bottom); Mary Evans Picture Library/The Image Works: p. 22; Betsy Dupuis/istock International: Rosie the Riveter icon; Martin Bond/Photo Researchers, Inc.: p. 14, p. 28; Mary Evans/Photo Researchers, Inc.: p. 30; Simon Fraser/Photo Researchers, Inc.: p. 29 (right); Doug Martin/Photo Researchers, Inc.: p. 10; Tom McHugh/Photo Researchers, Inc.: p. 25 (bottom); Charles D. Winters/Photo Researchers, Inc.: p. 1, p. 11 (bottom); Reuters/Mario Anzuoni: p. 18 (bottom); Reuters/Str Old: p. 26; Reuters/Tim Wimborne: p. 25 (top); Other Images from stock CD.

Illustrations: Rob MacGregor: p. 9, p. 16

Cover: Fuel cell vehicles are on the road today, although they are too expensive to be sold at car dealerships. A number of countries, such as Iceland, Canada, the United States, and England used fuel cell buses in their public transportation system.

Title page: Electrolyzers are devices that perform electrolysis, the breaking up of water into hydrogen gas and oxygen gas. This picture is of a simple device called the Hoffman apparatus, which demonstrates electrolysis. The bubbles in one test tube are hydrogen gas, while the bubbles in the other tube are oxygen.

Library and Archives Canada Cataloguing in Publication

Walker, Niki, 1972-
    Hydrogen : running on water / Niki Walker.

(Energy revolution)
Includes index.
ISBN-13: 978-0-7787-2915-0 (bound)
ISBN-10: 0-7787-2915-X (bound)
ISBN-13: 978-0-7787-2929-7 (pbk.)
ISBN-10: 0-7787-2929-X (pbk.)

    1. Hydrogen as fuel--Juvenile literature. I. Title. II. Series.

TP359.H8W34 2006   j665.8'1   C2006-902465-0

Library of Congress Cataloging-in-Publication Data

Walker, Niki, 1972-
    Hydrogen : running on water / written by Niki Walker.
      p. cm. -- (Energy revolution)
    Includes index.
    ISBN-13: 978-0-7787-2915-0 (rlb)
    ISBN-10: 0-7787-2915-X (rlb)
    ISBN-13: 978-0-7787-2929-7 (pbk)
    ISBN-10: 0-7787-2929-X (pbk)
    1. Hydrogen as fuel--Juvenile literature. I. Title. II. Series.
    TP359.H8W35 2006
    665.8'1--dc22
                           2006014369

Crabtree Publishing Company

www.crabtreebooks.com   1-800-387-7650

Published in Canada
Crabtree Publishing
616 Welland Ave.
St. Catharines, ON
L2M 5V6

Published in the United States
Crabtree Publishing
PMB16A
350 Fifth Ave., Suite 3308
New York, NY 10118

Published in the United Kingdom
Crabtree Publishing
White Cross Mills
High Town, Lancaster
LA1 4XS

Published in Australia
Crabtree Publishing
386 Mt. Alexander Rd.
Ascot Vale (Melbourne)
VIC 3032

Contents

Energy Conservation: 'We Can Do It!'

"We Can Do It" was a slogan that appeared on posters made during World War II. One poster featured "Rosie the Riveter," a woman dressed in blue coveralls (shown below). The poster was originally intended to encourage women to enter the workforce in industry to replace the men who left to serve in the war. Today, the image of Rosie the Riveter represents a time when people came together as a society to reach a common goal. Today's energy challenge can be combatted in a similar way. Together, we can work to save our planet from the pollution caused by burning fossil fuels by learning to conserve energy and developing alternative energy sources.

Everyday Energy

Energy makes everything from living things to machines, function. Plants and animals get energy from food and use it to move and grow. Most cars run on the energy they get from gasoline, while many other machines and devices, such as refrigerators and light switches, use energy they get from **electricity**.

Energy Carriers

An energy carrier moves energy from place to place. Electricity is the main energy carrier used today. Most electricity is made at **power plants** by burning fossil fuels, such as oil or coal. Electricity can also be made using **nuclear energy**. Electricity is sent over power lines to provide energy to homes and businesses.

Hydrogen as a Carrier

Hydrogen is a colorless, odorless **gas**. It is also an energy carrier, which means that it can store energy and deliver it to where it is needed. When it is burned, hydrogen produces heat. It is also used to power fuel cells, which are devices similar to batteries that produce electricity. Hydrogen is moved to where it is needed in pipelines, trucks, or ships. Scientists and governments believe hydrogen will be an important energy carrier in the future.

(below) Electricity is produced from an energy source, which includes fossil fuels, the wind, and the Sun. Some ways of creating electricity pollute the environment, such as using coal.

4

Power Sources

An energy source provides the energy from which electricity or hydrogen is created. Energy sources are either non-renewable or renewable. Non-renewable sources include fossil fuels, such as coal, oil, and natural gas. There is a limited amount of these energy sources. Renewable sources, also called alternative energy sources, are continually replaced, either by people or by nature. These include the Sun, wind, and biomass. Renewable energy sources do not create harmful gases that pollute the environment.

Solar power, or energy from the Sun, is an alternative energy source.

(bottom right) Car companies are creating designs for vehicles powered by fuel cells. Fuel cells use hydrogen to create the electricity that powers the cars' motors.

Conservation Tip

Energy conservation means limiting the amount of power that we use. You can find tips on how to conserve energy, and facts about energy conservation in boxes like these.

Time for Change

Today, most energy comes from fossil fuels. When fossil fuels are burned, the energy they have stored in them is released. At the same time, gases that harm the environment and people's health are also created. Once the world's supply of fossil fuels have been used up, they cannot be replaced. Using alternative energy, such as wind and solar power, provide unlimited energy that does not pollute the environment.

(above) A police officer directs traffic while engulfed in exhaust fumes from fossil fuel burning vehicles. Vehicle exhaust, or waste gases, creates smog, which is a blanket of air pollution that hangs low in the sky over many cities and causes breathing problems.

Global Warming

Many scientists believe burning fossil fuels is a major cause of global warming. Global warming is the gradual rise in temperature of Earth's **atmosphere** and oceans. When fossil fuels are burned as fuel to power cars or heat homes, they release greenhouse gases, such as carbon dioxide. Greenhouse gases trap the Sun's heat in the atmosphere and warm up the planet. Scientists believe global warming will cause major problems, such as melting the ice at the North and South poles, causing ocean levels to rise and flooding coastal areas where millions of people live. It will also affect weather around the world and cause more intense storms, such as hurricanes and tornadoes. Using alternative energy, and burning fewer fossil fuels will slow global warming.

Energy Out of Control

Fossil fuels are found only in certain areas of the world, which means that not every country has its own supply. Most countries have to buy fossil fuels, such as oil, from other countries. As the supply of fossil fuels decreases, their price will rise, making it more expensive to power cars and heat homes. To ensure that people have a steady supply of energy that they can afford, countries need to use more alternative energy, such as wind and solar energy. Fuel cells, which use hydrogen, are a technology that could one day provide non-polluting renewable energy. By making hydrogen safe, easy, and inexpensive to use, most countries may someday be able to produce all of their own energy.

(above) Oil is moved across oceans in large ships called tankers. Tankers sometimes crash or leak, and their contents spill into the water. These leaks harm or kill fish, seabirds, and other animals, which get coated in oil.

(below) Oil is a valuable energy source because it can be made into products such as gasoline. Much of the world's oil is imported, or brought in, from oil fields in the Middle East, such as this one in Saudi Arabia.

What is Hydrogen?

Hydrogen is a colorless, odorless, gas that exists in nature. Many substances on Earth are partly made up of hydrogen. For example, water is made up of hydrogen and oxygen, a gas that makes up a large part of the air we breathe. Hydrogen can be used to store and carry energy from one place to another. In the future, hydrogen along with alternative energy sources could provide most of the energy people use.

Forms of Hydrogen

Hydrogen is the most common gas in the universe. The Sun and other stars are made up mostly of hydrogen. On Earth, hydrogen is found in combination with other substances, such as in water. Most of Earth's hydrogen supply is in water. When hydrogen is removed from the substance it is combined with, it can then be used as an energy carrier.

Fossil fuels, such as oil, contain hydrogen. Fossil fuels are called hydrocarbons, which means that they are made up of hydrogen and carbon. Here, oil is being drilled from beneath the ocean floor.

NORTH CORMORANT

Hydrogen Up Close

Hydrogen, like everything else on Earth, is made up of atoms. Atoms are tiny particles of matter that are too small to see. Atoms bond, or join, with other atoms to make other liquids or gases. Hydrogen atoms bond with oxygen atoms to make water. Hydrogen atoms also bond with carbon atoms to make fossil fuels. Before hydrogen can be used, it has to be freed by breaking the bonds that hold the atoms together.

Inside an Atom

Atoms are made up of even smaller parts called neutrons, protons, and electrons. Hydrogen atoms are the smallest, simplest atoms. They have only one proton and one electron. Atoms often bond together by sharing electrons. The illustration below shows the structure of a single hydrogen atom.

proton

electron

nucleus

neutron

The center of an atom is called the nucleus. A hydrogen nucleus is made up of one proton and one neutron. A proton has a small positive electric charge. A neutron has no charge.

Electrons have a small negative electric charge. They orbit, or circle, the nucleus. They are held in their orbits because their negative charge attracts them to the positive charge of the nucleus, similar to the way magnets work.

Conservation Tip

You can conserve energy and reduce pollution by walking, riding your bike, or using public transit. Cars and trucks use energy they get from fossil fuels, which creates a lot of pollution. Driving less is one way to cut this pollution. Public transit carries many people to the same place, therefore reducing the number of vehicles on the road. If you have to drive, try carpooling with friends.

Freeing Hydrogen

Breaking the bonds that hold hydrogen atoms together with other atoms requires energy. There are several ways to produce hydrogen.

Conservation Tip

It takes energy, often from burning fossil fuels, to make commercial fertilizers. Instead of buying fertilizers at the store, make your own fertilizer by composting. Composting is when organic, or once living, matter, such as vegetable scraps and yard waste, rots. The material that remains can then be used to fertilize plants.

Natural Gas Reforming

Natural gas reforming is the most common way to produce hydrogen because it is the least expensive and produces the most hydrogen. Natural gas is a fossil fuel, which means it is made up of hydrocarbons. During a process called steam reforming, natural gas is combined with hot steam. Steam is water in gas form. The bonds holding together atoms in the steam and in the natural gas break. The atoms shuffle around, forming new bonds and new substances, including hydrogen and other gases.

Today, one of the main uses for hydrogen is in fertilizers, which are used to help plants grow.

Gasifying Coal

Many hydrogen producing plants, or factories, around the world use coal gasification to make hydrogen. Gasification is the process of turning a solid substance into a gas, usually by using intense heat. To turn coal into a gas, it is heated to very high temperatures, around 1652° F (900° C), and is mixed with steam and oxygen. The gas that is produced is made up mainly of **carbon monoxide,** carbon dioxide, and hydrogen. The hydrogen is separated from the rest of the gas and stored. Coal gasification is the oldest way of producing hydrogen. It is more expensive than producing hydrogen from natural gas reforming and releases much more carbon dioxide that pollutes the air.

(below) This simple-looking device is called a Hoffman apparatus. It uses electricity, supplied by the battery, to break water down into hydrogen and oxygen gases.

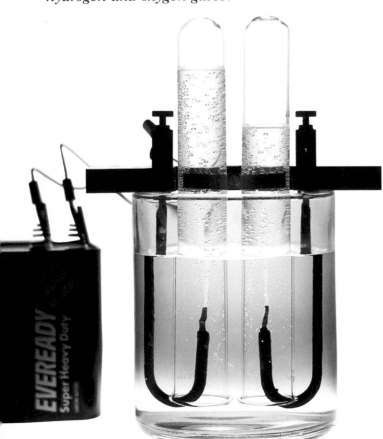

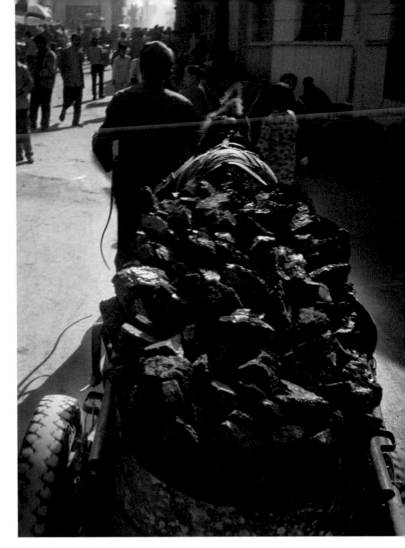

(above) Coal is a fossil fuel that has been burned as an energy source for thousands of years. Burning coal pollutes the environment, but it is still done, especially in poorer countries where coal is plentiful and cheap.

Fuel From Water

Electrolysis uses electricity to split water into hydrogen and oxygen atoms. When electricity is sent through water, it breaks the bonds that hold the oxygen and hydrogen atoms together. The hydrogen gas that is formed is then captured and stored. Today, very little hydrogen is produced using electrolysis. Electrolyzers, or devices that carry out electrolysis, use electricity, which is expensive. Hydrogen produced by electrolysis costs up to three times more than producing hydrogen from natural gas.

Biomass Gas

Hydrogen can also be made by gasifying biomass. Biomass is the name for all living things on Earth and their waste. Grasses, wood chips, sawdust, and animal dung are all examples of biomass. Biomass is heated to high temperatures until it breaks down into a gas. Steam is added to the gas to produce hydrogen and carbon dioxide. Biomass is a renewable source of energy, but it also releases carbon dioxide into the air. Much of this carbon dioxide is in turn taken in by growing plants that use the gas to help them grow.

(below) Scientists are studying a way to collect hydrogen made by pond scum, or algae. When algae grows, it produces small amounts of hydrogen. Currently, scientists are not collecting enough hydrogen to make it worth the cost.

(above) Wind farms generate electricity that is sent over power lines to homes and businesses. Sometimes more energy is made than what is needed. In the future, this extra energy could power electrolyzers to produce hydrogen.

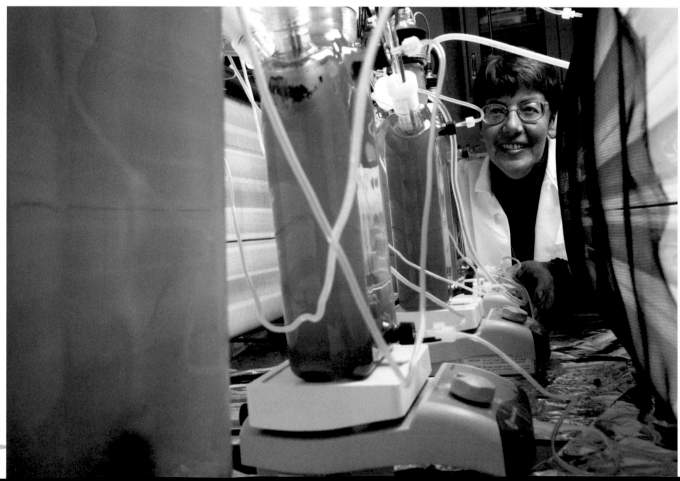

Reaching Customers

Once hydrogen has been freed from other substances, it is transported to where it is needed. Moving hydrogen is a challenge. Special equipment is used because hydrogen leaks easily, and it makes most metals and plastics brittle, or breakable. Today, some hydrogen is transported using pipelines, which are networks of metal pipes that run below or above ground and carry fuels across long distances. There are some hydrogen pipelines in the United States and Europe, although there are many more that transport fossil fuels. Hydrogen is also transported by trucks, trains, and ships.

(above) This fueling station in Washington D.C. offers both gasoline and hydrogen gas. The station was the first of its kind in North America. It opened in 2004.

Hydrogen On-site

One solution to the problem of delivering hydrogen is to produce it on-site, or at the place it will be used, such as at a fueling station. Today, there are a few hydrogen fueling stations in the world that produce hydrogen on-site using electrolyzers or natural gas reforming. They are found in California, Japan, Germany, Holland, Spain, Iceland, and Sweden.

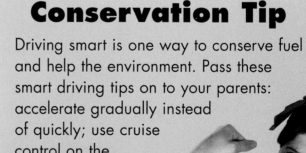

Conservation Tip

Driving smart is one way to conserve fuel and help the environment. Pass these smart driving tips on to your parents: accelerate gradually instead of quickly; use cruise control on the highway; ensure that your car's tires are properly inflated; and replace your car's air filter regularly.

13

Storing Power

Hydrogen can be stored as a gas, liquid, or solid. As with many fuels, hydrogen is flammable, or can easily catch fire. Scientists are looking for safe and easy ways to store hydrogen.

Under Pressure

Hydrogen is a diffuse gas, which means it is light and spreads out quickly, taking up a lot of room. To make using hydrogen more efficient, it is compressed, or has its atoms packed more closely together. Compressed hydrogen is stored in strong, tightly sealed tanks. This is because hydrogen gas leaks through the tiniest holes and can pass through some solid materials. A hydrogen tank used to power a car is about ten times bigger than a gasoline tank used to store the same amount of energy.

Hydrides

Hydrogen can also be stored in a solid form, such as a powder. Mixing hydrogen with one or more types of metal is called a hydride. The metals in a hydride powder absorb hydrogen, much like sponges absorb water. The hydrogen atoms bond with the atoms that make up the metal. To break the bonds and release the hydrogen, the metal is heated. Hydrides are much safer than gas or liquid hydrogen, but they are also very heavy, which makes them unsuitable for powering vehicles. Scientists are working to develop new, lightweight hydrides to solve this problem.

(right) Fueling a vehicle with hydrogen gas is different than fueling with gasoline. A hydrogen pump's nozzle has to be completely sealed around the tank's opening, or the gas will escape.

Hydrogen Rocket Fuel

The National Aeronautics and Space Administration (NASA), in the United States, is the world's biggest user of hydrogen. Since the late 1950s, NASA has used liquid hydrogen as a fuel to launch its rockets and space shuttles. It takes a lot of liquid hydrogen to launch shuttles. When the shuttle lifts off, it carries 227,800 pounds (103,330 kilograms) of liquid hydrogen in its external fuel tank! NASA's hydrogen is produced when natural gas is reformed and then liquified. The liquid hydrogen is shipped by tanker truck to the Kennedy Space Center in Florida.

Hydrogen is stored in a massive 850,000 gallon (3,217,590 liter) tank on a corner of NASA's shuttle launch pad.

Liquid Hydrogen

Hydrogen gas can also be cooled and stored in liquid form. Liquids are more dense, or have more closely packed atoms, than gases. This means that hydrogen in liquid form stores more energy than it does in gas form. Hydrogen gas turns to liquid at temperatures below -423° F (-252° C). Liquid hydrogen is made in factories using special refrigeration and compression equipment. It is very expensive to make because the machines require a lot of energy to run, and the storage tanks have to be specially made to keep the hydrogen cold.

Conservation Tip

Energy is used to make every product we use in our day to day lives. It takes energy to manufacture, advertise, and to transport these products. Keep this in mind when buying products. Buy recycled products when possible. Buy products that do not use a lot of packaging. If there is a lot of packaging, try to make sure it is recyclable.

Fuel Cells

Fuel cells are devices that turn hydrogen into electricity. Fuel cells can power anything that uses electricity, from cellular phones to home appliances to cars and trucks. Fuel cells do not create any pollution. Besides electricity, the only thing fuel cells make is water.

Pure and Simple

A fuel cell runs on the oxygen that is in the air and the hydrogen that is stored in a container. The container may be a small cartridge if it is powering a laptop computer or cellular phone, or a large tank for powering cars. Even larger tanks are used for fuel cells that provide electricity to a building.

How Fuel Cells Work

1 A fuel cell looks like a flat thin panel. Hydrogen enters on one side, while oxygen enters on the other.

Hydrogen

Membrane

Water

Oxygen

2 After the hydrogen atoms enter the fuel cell, they are stripped of their electrons. The electrons flow out of the fuel cell along a wire. This flow of electrons is electricity.

3 The wire is attached to an electric device, such as a light bulb, and the electricity flowing through the wire provides the energy needed to run the device.

4 Hydrogen atoms cross the membrane and bond with the oxygen atoms on the other side. They form water.

Endless Cycle

By using electrolysis and fuel cells, people can create an endless cycle of non-polluting energy. The cycle is repeated, as the water produced by fuel cells gets split by electrolysis to produce hydrogen. The hydrogen then powers fuel cells, which in turn produce more water.

(right) Since the 1960s, fuel cells have provided electricity for all of NASA's spacecraft. The fuel cells power equipment while producing pure water for the astronauts to drink.

(left) There are several types of fuel cells being developed today. Each type is made from different materials and produces different amounts of electricity, which makes them more ideal to run certain products. Fuel cells can power everything from cellular phones, to laptop computers and vehicle engines. This toy Godzilla robot is even powered by a fuel cell.

17

Portable Power

Fuel cells are similar to batteries. Both create electricity and both are portable, or can be moved from place to place. A battery has a limited amount of fuel, which is stored inside it as chemicals. When its fuel is used up, a battery dies. It needs to be replaced or recharged for several hours. When fuel cells run out of hydrogen, the tank or cartridge that supplies them is refilled or replaced. Fuel cells run much longer than batteries before they need to be refueled with hydrogen, and they can be refueled again and again.

Cell Stacks

A single fuel cell can produce as little as one **watt** of electricity, which can be enough to power some small devices such as cellular phones or digital cameras. For jobs that require a lot of electricity, such as running a car or powering a building, fuel cells are joined together to form a fuel stack. Fuel stacks can combine any number of cells to create the amount of power needed.

(right) This cellular phone is being charged by a fuel cell. The cylinder being inserted is the source of hydrogen.

(below) This fuel cell stack is made of dozens of fuel cells. Each vertical gray column, or panel, is one hydrogen fuel cell.

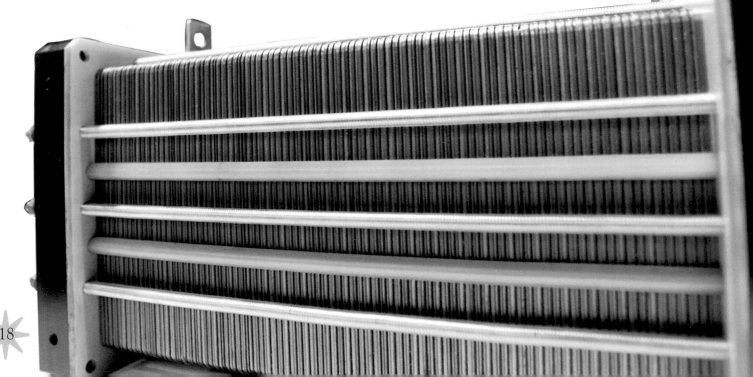

18

Stay-put Power

Fuel cells can also be used for stationary power. Stationary power is a source of electricity that stays in one place, such as a power plant. A stationary fuel cell stack can provide all the electricity a home or business needs. In the future, huge stacks may even power all the buildings in towns and cities! Fuel cell stacks are also useful as backup power for homes and businesses that usually get electricity from the **power grid**. If there is a **blackout**, fuel cells connected directly to the building can provide electricity to keep computers, appliances, and other devices running. Today, fuel cell stacks provide stationary power for some banks, military bases, police stations, and office buildings.

In 2005, the Sheraton New York Hotel & Towers became the first hotel in New York City to install a fuel cell power plant to help supply the hotel's electricity needs.

Conservation Tip

Recycling is an important way to help the Earth, but even the recycling process requires energy. Reuse recyclable products, such as paper bags, and aluminum foil, pans, and plates until they cannot be used again, then toss them in the recycle bin.

On the Road

Emissions from cars, sport utility vehicles, or SUVs, trucks, and other vehicles are one of the major causes of pollution. Many car companies, governments, and scientists are developing vehicles that create little or no pollution, including cars powered by hydrogen. Hydrogen can be burned in engines, or it can be used to power fuel cells that run electric motors.

Burning Hydrogen

Almost all cars and trucks are powered by **internal combustion engines** that burn gasoline or diesel fuel. These engines can be modified, or changed, to burn hydrogen instead of gasoline. Burning hydrogen in internal combustion engines does not release carbon dioxide into the air, but it does produce a greenhouse gas called nitrous oxide. The amount of greenhouse gases released by hydrogen internal combustion engines, or HICEs, is about 99 percent less than engines that burn gasoline.

More than half of all the fossil fuels people burn are used to power cars, trucks, and other vehicles.

(right) Carmakers such as Ford, BMW, and Mazda, are developing cars with hydrogen internal combustion engines (HICEs). The engines can run on hydrogen, gasoline, or a combination of the two fuels. Some people believe that HICE cars will be a big step toward switching from fossil fuel to hydrogen power.

Get on the Bus

In 1993, Ballard Power Systems, a Canadian company that develops fuel cells, put the first fuel cell powered bus on the road. They wanted to show the world that fuel cells could power vehicles. The bus ran in Vancouver, Canada, as part of the city's public transit system. A public bus was a good vehicle to choose because thousands of people ride it every day, and a bus can carry a large tank of hydrogen that would be too big and heavy for a smaller vehicle. In the years since this first hydrogen bus demonstration, fuel cell companies have continued to improve and test fuel cells for vehicles. Today, there are more than a hundred public fuel cell buses operating in cities in the United States, Canada, Europe, Japan, Brazil, Mexico, China, Egypt, India, and Iceland.

Test Driving Fuel Cells

Carmakers have been working on fuel cell cars for many years, and have put many vehicles on the road for trials and demonstrations. Fuel cell cars are extremely expensive, so they are not yet sold through car dealerships. Many people are confident that fuel cell cars will be available for sale to everyone by 2020, but there are many challenges that need to be overcome first, such as building more hydrogen fueling stations and lowering the price of fuel cell vehicles.

This motorcycle, called the ENV, was the first to run on a hydrogen fuel cell. First unveiled in London, England, in 2005, the motorcycle travels about 100 miles (160 kilometers) on a single tank of hydrogen.

Hydrogen's History

Hydrogen was discovered in 1766 by an English scientist named Henry Cavendish. He called it "inflammable air," which means "air that catches fire." Since its discovery, scientists and inventors have found various ways to use hydrogen.

Up, Up, and Away

On December 1, 1783, Jacques Charles and Nicolas Robert became the first to travel in a hydrogen balloon, which Charles invented. Hydrogen is lighter than air, so the balloons lifted up without needing to heat the gas, as **hot air balloons** did. This made hydrogen balloons safer, as fire was thought to no longer be a danger. Hydrogen balloons could also stay in the air longer and travel farther than hot air balloons. Balloons became popular attractions at fairs and public celebrations.

Town Gas

In the 1800s, a type of gas called town gas was used in people's homes for cooking and lighting. Town gas was made by heating coal, and was a mixture of hydrogen and other gases. Most people stopped using town gas in the early 1900s, when vast amounts of natural gas were found in North America and Europe. Natural gas became more popular because it produces more heat and does not create soot or smoke like town gas. Town gas is still used in some parts of Asia, where natural gas is unavailable or too expensive.

In the 1800s and early 1900s, hydrogen balloons were used during wars, including World War I. They offered army leaders a good view of enemy positions.

The Age of Airships

Improvements in hydrogen balloons led to the invention of steerable balloons, called airships. Henri Giffard built the first airship in 1852 by attaching a small steam engine and propeller to a hydrogen balloon. In 1900, Ferdinand von Zeppelin, a German military officer, developed a new airship, known as a dirigible, or zeppelin. The dirigible had a metal frame covered with a fabric "skin." During the 1930s, zeppelins carried thousands of passengers between Germany and North and South America. A flight between Germany and the United States usually took three to four days.

The *Hindenburg* Disaster

The age of airships ended suddenly in 1937, when the world's largest zeppelin, the *Hindenburg*, exploded. As the *Hindenburg* approached the docking tower, it burst into flames. The airship burned up and crashed in 32 seconds. Thirty-six people died. At the time, people blamed the hydrogen in the balloon for the explosion. No one wanted to travel using hydrogen anymore. Recently, some scientists have shown that while the hydrogen did ignite, it did not cause the disaster. The *Hindenburg*'s fabric skin was coated in the same chemicals used in today's rocket fuel. Many people believe a spark of **static electricity** from a lightning storm set the fabric on fire, causing an explosion.

The Hindenburg *airship crashed in Lakehurst, New Jersey.*

23

The First Fuel Cells

The first fuel cell was invented by British scientist William Grove in 1839. The earliest fuel cells worked in the same basic way as today's fuel cells, by combining hydrogen and oxygen to produce electricity and water. Unfortunately, the cells produced little electricity, and hydrogen was difficult and expensive to produce. By the early 1900s, people in Europe and America had reliable, inexpensive electricity from coal and **hydropower plants**, so few people continued to develop fuel cell technology.

Fuel Cells Find a Use

In 1959, Francis T. Bacon made the first fuel cell that was powerful enough to run a machine. At the time, NASA was searching for a reliable power source for its spacecraft, and was impressed by Bacon's fuel cell. The cell not only produced electricity, but also water and heat for the astronauts to use. NASA began using fuel cells in the 1960s. For decades, NASA was the only major customer for fuel cells because they were so much more expensive than other power sources, such as gasoline.

Francis T. Bacon was a British engineer who built the first fuel cell powerful enough to run machines. The first device powered by his fuel cell was a welding machine, a device that joins pieces of metal together.

The 1973 Oil Crisis

In the 1960s, companies began developing fuel cells for cars, but the fuel cells could not compete with internal combustion engines, which were far less expensive to run. The gasoline that powered most car engines was made from oil imported from Middle Eastern countries. In 1973, these countries refused to sell oil to the United States and European countries. The demand for oil was far greater than what was available, which caused prices to soar.

(right) Hydrogen is still used in some balloons today. Scientists send hydrogen balloons into the atmosphere to collect weather information. The balloons travel up to 25 miles (40 kilometers) into the atmosphere!

(above) Gasoline was very expensive during the 1973 oil crisis. Many gas stations ran out of gasoline to sell.

Seeing the Future

As a result of the oil crisis, governments began to look into ways to reduce their country's dependence on oil. They gave money to companies developing alternative energy sources, such as fuel cells. Many companies began developing better and less expensive fuel cells, but people lost interest in hydrogen and alternative energy sources when the price of oil and gasoline dropped in the 1980s. In the past few years, governments and people around the world have once again become interested in fuel cells and hydrogen, because they hope they can help reduce global warming and dependence on other countries for oil.

The Obstacles

Many people believe that hydrogen is the fuel of the future. There are many challenges with hydrogen and its use that need to be solved before it can become a main source of power.

Fear of Fire

There is a risk of fire and explosion with all fuels, but hydrogen can be ignited more easily than gasoline or natural gas. A hydrogen fire can be started by sparks from electric equipment or static electricity, or if it comes in contact with extremely hot objects. It is also almost impossible to detect a hydrogen leak because hydrogen has no smell, color, or taste. People who support the switch to hydrogen believe the dangers can be avoided if people follow safety rules just as they follow rules to safely use gasoline. They also argue that, in some ways, hydrogen is safer than liquid fuels. Hydrogen gas rises quickly. It does not take long for the threat of a fire to disappear as the hydrogen spreads out.

Help or Hindrance?

Today, most hydrogen comes from fossil fuels and producing it only adds to pollution and global warming. Producing hydrogen from clean energy sources is an important goal, and may be possible in the future after more solar power plants, and other renewable energy sources are built - a task that takes a lot of time, money, and planning.

This cigarette-shaped balloon is filled with hydrogen. Ignited to mark World No Smoking Day, the hydrogen rises and the flame gives off almost no heat.

No Network

If hydrogen is to become the fuel of the future, hydrogen plants, pipelines, and fueling stations must be built. Today, fossil fuels are the main source of energy and they are readily available to customers. Pipelines and tankers move oil to refineries where it is made into gasoline. The gasoline gets shipped to gas stations and other customers using pipelines and tanker trucks. Gas stations are found in every town and city. This network, or groups of people and companies, that moves oil and gas to customers around the world, is known as an infrastructure. Today, there is only a small network for producing and moving hydrogen. It links the few hydrogen plants in the world to the few hydrogen customers. Experts believe building a hydrogen network will take time and a lot of money.

(below) Before people will buy cars fueled by hydrogen, they must believe they are safe and affordable. Today, fuel cell cars cost much more than cars powered by gasoline. There are also few fueling stations that sell hydrogen gas.

CASE STUDY

Forcing Change

The state of California has created laws that are meant to slow down global warming. The state is making car companies produce vehicles that create far less pollution than those on the road today. Carmakers have until 2009 to come up with ways to meet the demands of the state. Fuel cell cars can meet these demands. In April 2004, the governor of California promised that by 2010, there will be hydrogen fueling stations on all major highways in the state. The government has promised to share the cost of building the first few stations and has agreed to buy fuel cell cars for government workers. By helping build fueling stations and buying hydrogen cars, the government hopes to encourage the change from fossil fuels to hydrogen.

Making the Change

In the future, many countries may switch to a hydrogen **economy**. In a hydrogen economy, factories, homes, cars, and other machines will be powered by hydrogen that is made from clean, renewable energy sources. Making the switch from fossil fuels to other energy sources cannot happen overnight. It will require planning, time, and a lot of money.

The First Step

This first step to creating hydrogen economies has already begun. Scientists are working on better, cheaper fuel cells and less expensive ways to make and store hydrogen. Governments and companies are spending billions of dollars to help pay for this research. Many governments are also creating laws to reduce the amount of fossil fuels businesses and individuals use, which will encourage people to use more renewable energy. During this first step, hydrogen will come from fossil fuels such as natural gas, gasoline, and coal. Over time, more electricity will be produced using alternative energy sources, and this electricity can be used to produce hydrogen without pollution.

The Next Steps

In order for a hydrogen economy to become a reality, everyone has to get involved. The major change will come when people decide to buy cars, laptop computers, cameras, and other devices that run on hydrogen fuel cells. Governments can encourage people to buy fuel cell cars and stationary fuel cells to power their homes and businesses by offering grants and rebates, or money back, to those who buy. As more people buy hydrogen-powered products, the prices will come down, making it affordable and allowing the hydrogen economy to grow over time.

This house in Germany is run using solar energy and a fuel cell. Hydrogen gas is stored in the large white tank.

Iceland's New Economy

Iceland, an island country in the North Atlantic Ocean, is planning to have the world's first hydrogen economy by 2050. Iceland is an ideal place for a hydrogen economy because most of its power comes from geothermal energy, a non-polluting form of energy. Icelanders use this energy to heat buildings and produce electricity. The idea to switch to hydrogen was introduced in the 1970s when the oil crisis struck. It was not until 1999 that a group called Icelandic New Energy (INE) formed, which brings together the Icelandic government with businesses and people that can help make a hydrogen economy in Iceland a reality. Companies involved include DaimlerChrysler, a car company that develops hydrogen cars, Norsk Hydro, which provides electrolyzers, the machines that electrolyze water to produce hydrogen, and Shell Hydrogen, which builds hydrogen fueling stations. One of the world's first public hydrogen fueling stations opened in Iceland's capital, Reykjavik, in 2003, and today, three hydrogen buses are a part of their public transit system.

Iceland has enough geothermal energy to produce all the hydrogen it needs. Geothermal energy is heat from deep inside the Earth that escapes through volcanoes, hot springs, and geysers. The people above are swimming in a hot spring outside a geothermal power station.

Timeline

Hydrogen may be the fuel of the future, but it also has a long and rich past. Many of the discoveries and inventions made in the past 250 years have paved the way for the hydrogen technology of today and tomorrow.

c. 1500

Early chemist Theophrastus Bombastus von Hohenheim produces hydrogen by mixing acids and metals. He does not realize that the gas is hydrogen.

1766

Henry Cavendish discovers hydrogen. He later produces water by touching a spark of electricity to hydrogen gas.

1783

Jacques Charles launches the first unmanned hydrogen balloon. Later that year, he and his assistant are the first to fly in a hydrogen balloon.

1800

British scientists William Nicholson and Anthony Carlisle learn that water can be split into hydrogen and oxygen using electrolysis.

1838

German scientist Christian Schonbein has the idea that combining hydrogen and oxygen could create an electric current and water - the idea behind fuel cells.

1843

William Grove creates the first fuel cell.

1874

Science fiction writer Jules Verne writes of hydrogen as a fuel of the future in his book, *The Mysterious Island*. Many of his ideas are coming true today.

1889

Ludwig Mon and Charles Langer give fuel cells their name.

Antoine Lavoisier, a French chemist, named hydrogen in 1783.

1937

The *Hindenburg* disaster ends the popularity of airships and leads people to believe that hydrogen is a dangerous gas.

1959

Francis T. Bacon demonstrates the world's first practical fuel cell. Later that year, the Allis Chalmers Manufacturing Company demonstrates a fuel cell tractor—the world's first fuel cell vehicle.

1990

The first solar-powered plant for producing hydrogen opens in Germany.

1993

Ballard Power Systems begins testing fuel cell buses in Vancouver. The test is a success.

1998

Iceland reveals its plan to be the first country with a hydrogen economy.

2000

Ballard Power Systems introduces the first fuel cell ready for use in cars.

2004

California is the first state to promise to build a "hydrogen highway." By 2010, the state wants hydrogen filling stations on all major highways.

2005

A family in southern California becomes the first to have a fuel cell car. They are taking part in testing the vehicle.

(above) During the 1960s, NASA used fuel cells to power the Apollo rockets, and liquid hydrogen as the fuel for launching rockets.

(below) In 2004, Germany tested the world's first fuel cell submarine.

31

Glossary

algae A group of plants, including seaweeds, that do not have flowers, roots, or stems

atmosphere The layers of gases that surround Earth

atoms The smallest building blocks that make up living and non-living things

biomass Organic, or once living, matter that can be used for fuel

blackout A time when no electricity is running, often due to a storm, and lights, appliances, and other electric devices cannot be used

carbon A substance that is in many non-living and all living things

carbon monoxide A toxic gas that is flammable, and has no smell or color

economy How people in a country earn money, spend money, and use resources

electricity An electrical charge or current caused by a flow of electrons

gas A state of matter in which the parts of a substance are spread widely apart. Liquid and solid are two other states of matter

geyser A hot spring, or natural pool, that sends a column of water and steam into the air

hot air balloon An aircraft in which a large balloon is filled with heated air so it will rise up carrying its passengers in a basket, or gondola

hot spring A natural pool of warm water

hydropower plants A place that produces electricity using flowing water to turn a turbine; the turbine then powers a machine that generates electricity

internal combustion engine An engine, such as a car engine, that burns fuel and provides power

matter The substance from which all things are made. Anything that has mass and is liquid, solid, or gas

Middle East A large area made up of countries in northeast Africa and southeast Asia

nuclear energy A form of energy that does not create air pollution, but generates a harmful waste that must be safely stored for hundreds or thousands of years

power grid The system of power lines, generators, and other equipment that brings electricity to homes and other buildings

power plant A place that generates electricity

static electricity An electric charge that can cause sparks and is created by lightning or friction

watt A unit that is used to measure the amount of electricity a device uses or generates

World War I A war that took place largely on European soil between 1939 and 1945

Index

Printed in the U.S.A.